Amazing
Birds of Prey

WRITTEN BY
JEMIMA PARRY-JONES

PHOTOGRAPHED BY
MIKE DUNNING

DORLING KINDERSLEY
London · New York · Stuttgart

A Dorling Kindersley Book

Editor Bernadette Crowley
Art editor Mark Regardsoe
Managing editor Sophie Mitchell
Managing art editor Miranda Kennedy
Production Shelagh Gibson

Illustrations by Mark Iley and Julie Anderson
Birds supplied by The National Birds of Prey Centre, Newent, Gloucestershire
Special thanks to David Fung and James Pickford for research

First published in Great Britain in 1992 by
Dorling Kindersley Limited,
9 Henrietta Street, London, WC2E 8PS

A CIP catalogue record for this book
is available from the British Library

ISBN 0 86318 894 X

Colour reproduction by Colourscan, Singapore
Printed in Italy by A. Mondadori Editore, Verona

Contents

These children are about 1.2 m tall. They will show you the size of the birds in the main pictures.

What is a bird of prey?

Birds of prey are beautifully designed hunters. Unlike other birds, birds of prey catch their food – their prey – with their feet, which are often their killing tools. All birds of prey have hooked beaks which they use to tear into the animals they catch.

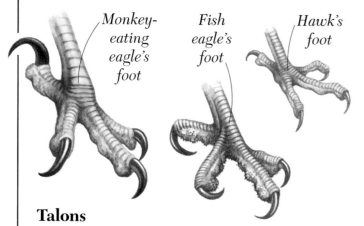

Monkey-eating eagle's foot

Fish eagle's foot

Hawk's foot

Talons

Birds of prey have four toes with curved claws called talons on each foot. Hawks have long, slim toes for catching birds in flight. Fish eagles have rough feet for holding slippery fish. Monkey-eating eagles have big, powerful feet for grabbing and crushing monkeys and other mammals.

What an eyeful!
Birds of prey have excellent eyesight. The eyes of the common buzzard are as big as your eyes – and it is only 50 cm tall! A buzzard could see you on the ground when you would need binoculars to see it flying above.

This is the life!
Many birds of prey catch enough food in one go to last them for a whole day. Because of this, they spend most of the time lazily watching the world go by.

Female

Male

Larger ladies
In most kinds of birds of prey, the female is larger than the male. Sometimes there is a big difference. The female Levant sparrowhawk can weigh twice as much as the male.

The staring eyes of the tawny eagle make it look fierce

Crop

Storing food

Birds of prey, except for owls, have a crop, a pouch where they can store food. The crop allows them to swallow more than they need at one go, and save it to eat later or to feed to their babies.

Napoleonic flag

People have used birds of prey as a symbol of strength and power since the earliest times. In the last century the French emperor Napoleon used an eagle on his flag.

Survival of the fittest

The tawny eagle, like other birds of prey, usually hunts sick or weak prey because they are easier to catch. This is of great value to the animal world as it means that only the strongest animals survive to breed strong youngsters.

Vultures

Vultures very rarely kill their own food. They prefer to eat other animals' left-overs or creatures that have simply dropped dead from old age.

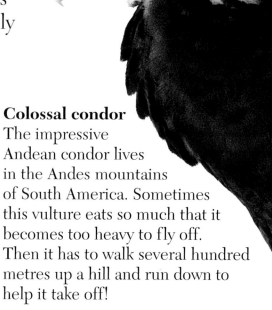

Sniffing vulture
The turkey vulture is the only bird of prey which uses a sense of smell to find food. It sniffs out dead animals in the South American jungle while flying very low over the treetops.

Colossal condor
The impressive Andean condor lives in the Andes mountains of South America. Sometimes this vulture eats so much that it becomes too heavy to fly off. Then it has to walk several hundred metres up a hill and run down to help it take off!

Ripped to shreds
Vultures have a strong beak. The lappet-faced vulture's beak is so strong that it can tear open the skin of a dead elephant. Other African vultures often have to wait for the lappet-faced vulture to arrive before they can start to feed.

Bath time
Vultures are very clean birds. After they have eaten, they often fly long distances to a river to have a bath.

A rare bird
The rarest vulture in the world is the California condor. None are left in the wild, but enough have now bred in captivity for breeders to begin releasing young ones back into the wild.

No more left-overs
The world needs vultures. They are the waste collectors of the bird world, speedily eating the flesh off dead animals before it has a chance to rot and cause disease.

The Andean condor has a wingspan of 3.5 m

Not just a pretty face
This amazing face belongs to the king vulture. A vulture has a bald head for a reason. The bird often has to dig deep into messy animal remains. If it had head and neck feathers, they would get very bloody, and the vulture would not be able to clean them with its beak.

Kites, harriers & ospreys

Kites are excellent flyers. A kite will often eat its prey in the air. Harriers hunt by flying slowly just above the ground, looking for small animals to eat. Ospreys fish for their food, so they live near water.

Follow that fire
Black kites often follow bush fires, looking for dead or dying insects and small mammals to eat.

Taking a dive
Ospreys fly high above the water when looking for fish. When they spot a victim, they dive towards it. Just before hitting the water, ospreys thrust their feet forwards, ready to grab the unlucky fish.

Rough feet
Sometimes when catching a fish the osprey will go completely underwater. Osprey's feet have spiky scales and long, curved talons to make sure slippery fish do not wriggle free.

Many mouths to feed
Some male harriers have two, or even three, female mates with chicks at one time. These male harriers have to work very hard to feed them all.

Food delivery
To save time, a male harrier does not bring food all the way to the nest. He calls to his mate and she flies out to meet him. He then drops the food and she catches it in her talons.

The African harrier hawk reaches into a tree hole

Baby snatcher
The African harrier hawk has unusual ankles which can bend forwards and backwards. It hunts by reaching into nests or holes and feeling around for eggs and small animals to eat.

Unwanted guest
Although kites hunt a great deal, they also eat food they have not caught themselves. Some cheeky kites have even been known to steal food from picnics!

Ankle

Hawks & falcons

Hawks and falcons are fierce hunters. Falcons dive towards their prey at speeds of over 160km/h. Hawks fly low over the ground in their search for food.

This is a young male peregrine falcon. He is 14 weeks old

Poisoned peregrines
Peregrine falcons almost died out recently. They ate birds which fed on grain that was sprayed with poisonous chemicals (for killing pests). Then the peregrine became poisoned too. Now these chemicals are banned and the peregrine population has grown.

Tangled web

The gabar goshawk nests high in the trees of Africa. To protect its nest of eggs from hungry enemies, it places a spider's web, complete with spider, on the nest. The spider weaves new webs, which hide the goshawk's nest.

Tree dweller

Forest falcons live in the dense rainforests of South America. When they hunt they have to fly with great skill to avoid crashing into trees or getting tangled up in branches.

Cook's favourite

In the Middle Ages, the goshawk was known as the "cook's bird". At that time, goshawks were trained to catch food for people. Goshawks hunt all sorts of creatures and cooks could fill their larder with the goshawk's catch.

Plucky bird

The sharp-shinned hawk feeds on small birds. Before eating a bird, the hawk takes it to a "plucking post", where the hawk plucks out its victim's feathers.

Tick picker

The yellow-headed caracara is a falcon from South America. It eats almost anything. It often sits on cattle and removes small insects called ticks which feed on the cattle's blood.

Pocket-sized

The smallest falcons are the pygmy falcons. The African pygmy falcon is only 15 cm tall. Not surprisingly, pygmy falcons feed on very small animals.

Eagles

Eagles are the most powerful of the birds of prey. They can even kill prey as big as themselves, using only their feet.

Big appetite
The martial eagle is the largest eagle in Africa. It usually hunts other birds, but this one has caught a small antelope. It must have been feeling hungry!

Young and bald
This young bald eagle is one year old. He will have to wait another four years before he gets his adult plumage. The bald eagle is the national emblem of the USA, where it stands for strength and freedom.

Easy prey
In winter, bald eagles gather beside rivers to catch salmon that have swum up the river to lay eggs. Pacific salmon die as soon as they lay their eggs and the eagles easily fish the dead salmon from the water.

Regal eagle
The harpy eagle, which can be up to 1 m tall, is known as the king of the eagles. It lives in the South American jungles. Its huge talons, which spread as wide as 23 cm, can easily crush its prey of monkeys and other tree-living animals.

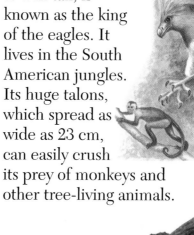

The adult bald eagle has white head feathers and dark brown body feathers

Socks or not

Eagles which hunt land animals have feathers all the way down to their toes. But eagles who hunt fish, such as white-bellied sea eagles, have bare legs so they don't have wet "socks" all day.

Circus act

The bateleur, an eagle from Africa, is a brilliant flyer. It can do the most amazing things in the air. It is well named – *bateleur* means "acrobat" or "tightrope walker" in French.

Feathers in his cap

Native Americans thought of the eagle as sacred. The greatest warriors, like this warrior from the Crow tribe, had eagle feathers in their war bonnets. Each feather stood for a brave deed.

Owls

Owls are sometimes called the muggers of the bird world. Their silent flight means that, often, their prey doesn't hear them coming – until it is too late!

White as snow
The snowy owl lives in the Arctic where there is snow all year round. It has a thick coat of snow-white feathers which keeps it warm. The snowy owl also has feathers on its feet. They act like slippers and keep its toes from getting frostbitten.

Wise old owl
Athene, the Greek goddess of wisdom, sometimes carried a little owl on her shoulder. She is often shown as having the head of an owl. This may be where the saying "wise old owl" comes from.

Rain stops play
Owls usually shelter from the rain to keep their soft feathers dry. But this barn owl has had to hunt in the rain because it has five hungry chicks to feed and cannot afford any time off.

Bird bullies
Other birds seem to fear owls, probably because owls sometimes hunt sleeping birds. If a group of birds sees an owl near their home, they may chase and mob it to drive the owl away from the area.

Down in one
Owls swallow most of their prey whole. An owl's mouth may look small, but it can open very wide indeed. This tawny owl chick looks very odd trying to swallow a large mouse whole.

An owl cannot move its huge eyes in their sockets. Instead, it swivels its head which can turn almost full-circle

Owls in love

Owls court by making lots of different sounds. Some loving couples even sing a duet, with each partner hooting its own tune. They also snuggle close together and touch beaks.

An owl has very soft feathers which allow it to fly silently

Night birds

The Bengal eagle owl lives in India where it hunts small animals such as lizards. Owls hunt mostly at night. Their eyesight and hearing are excellent and help them find prey in the dark. They see the world in black-and-white – not in colour.

Flight

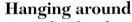

Most birds of prey have special flying skills. Their speedy swooping, swerving, and diving help them catch their prey.

Hanging around

Kestrels often hover, or stay flying in one spot, when hunting. Hovering is very hard work, but it means the kestrel can spot prey moving below it in tall grass.

Speeding bullet

Falcons fly the fastest when hunting. When diving towards prey, they fold up in the shape of a bullet and strike the prey, which falls to the ground. The falcon then flies down to grab its meal.

Vole attack

Once a hovering kestrel has spotted its prey, it dives at great speed and pounces on the surprised creature. This kestrel has caught a vole before the vole reached the safety of its burrow.

Falling in love

Bald eagles have a dramatic courtship flight. A mating pair will fly to a great height, lock talons, and then cartwheel downwards. They let go of each other just before reaching the ground.

Catching the sun

Birds take very good care of their feathers – they could not fly without them. This turkey vulture has just washed and is sunbathing to dry its feathers. The sun's rays are thought to help keep feathers in tiptop condition.

Pole position

This Harris's hawk is preparing to land. It has spread out its wing and tail feathers. This action makes it slow down to landing speed.

Long-distance lunch

Vultures will fly an enormous distance to a meal, sometimes over 160 km!

Tail feathers are spread out like a fan

Fussy eaters

Some birds of prey are particular about what they hunt; they will eat only certain types of food. These birds can be very fussy!

Broken bones
The bearded vulture has a taste for bones. It breaks the bones into bite-size portions by flying up high and dropping them on to rocks.

Going batty
Bat hawks eat bats – funnily enough! They hunt bats at dusk, when the bats wake up and start to come out for the night.

Snail snacks
The Everglade kite eats apple snails. Snails are hard to remove from their shell as they cling to the shell with a special muscle. The Everglade kite has a long, curved beak, which it eases into a snail shell, cuts this muscle, and pulls the snail out.

Plucking feathers
Peregrine falcons often eat only the best bits of an animal. This peregrine falcon has caught a pheasant for dinner but may eat only the juicy breast and leave the rest for somebody else. Like most birds of prey, it plucks the feathers off its catch before tucking in.

An Egyptian vulture about to smash an ostrich egg

Healthy eater

The palm nut vulture is an unusual bird of prey – its diet is mostly vegetarian. Sometimes it eats fish, but mostly it sits in an oil palm tree, munching palm nuts.

A smashing time!

The Egyptian vulture loves ostrich eggs, but its beak is not strong enough to break the tough shell. To get to the delicious inside of an ostrich egg, the vulture picks up a stone in its beak and chucks the stone at the egg to smash the shell.

Tough toes

Snake eagles have short, powerful toes which are perfect for catching slim and slithery snakes. Their legs are covered with large, tough scales. These scales protect the eagles against poisonous snakebites.

Early days

Most birds of prey do not lay many eggs at one time. It is hard work feeding hungry chicks with fresh meat every day. Birds of prey are attentive parents – they teach their young how to fly and hunt before the fully grown chicks leave home.

Golden eagle

Yellow-billed kite

Peregrine falcon

Saker falcon

Merlin

White-faced scops owl

African pygmy falcon

First comes the egg
Here are some bird-of-prey eggs. The largest of these, the golden eagle's, is 8 cm long; the smallest, the African pygmy falcon's, is 3 cm long.

King-size bed
Eagles build nests so big that an human adult could lie down in one. Most eagles return to the same nest each year to lay eggs and rear their young.

Feed me!
Bird-of-prey chicks, such as these red-tailed hawk chicks, are fed meat from birth. In a good year, all chicks are well-fed and grow strong. But some years there is not enough food around to feed the whole family. Then the strongest chicks get fed and the weaker ones die.

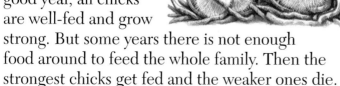

Interior designers
Red kites like to decorate their nests with wool and old bits of material. They have even been known to steal people's washing!

The fluffy fine feathers are called down

Thanks, honey!

Honey buzzards steal sections of wasp and bee nests to feed their chicks. These sections contain wasp and bee grubs which the chicks pick out and eat.

Fast growth

The African pygmy falcon is one of the smallest birds of prey. This African pygmy falcon chick is 14 days old and 7 cm tall. It has already grown halfway to its adult size and its adult flight feathers have started to grow.

City slickers

Even if you live in a city, you may still see birds of prey. Many kestrels and peregrine falcons live in cities. They nest on the ledges of high buildings, bridges, and churches.

Puffed out

If an animal threatens a long-eared owl and its chicks, the owl will fan out its wings and fluff up its feathers. This display by the owl makes it look big and frightening and may scare the enemy away.

Falconry

Falconry is the art of taming and training a bird of prey to hunt – not for itself but for its trainer, who is known as a falconer. Falconry is one of the oldest sports. It began in China about 4,000 years ago.

A hood stops the bird from getting frightened or overexcited

A falconry bird wears straps called jesses tied to its legs. The falconer uses jesses to hold on to the bird

Handy protection
This is a lanner falcon sitting on a falconer's hand. A thick glove is worn for the falconer's protection and the bird's comfort.

Battling bird

The Roman emperor Julius Caesar used falconry in battle. He trained birds of prey to kill pigeons which were carrying messages between his enemy's soldiers.

Hawking party

Hawking parties were great social occasions in the Middle Ages in Europe. People would dress splendidly and go for a day's hunting with their birds of prey.

Bath time

Falconry birds are given a bath every day. They also drink from their bathwater. Birds of prey drink very little and when they do it is called boozing.

Go fetch

Falconers use a dog, usually a pointer, to hunt with the bird. The dog frightens animals out of bushes and trees. Then the falconer removes the bird's hood, and the bird goes hunting.

Bell

Ring-a-ding

A falconry bird wears a bell, either on a leg or on the tail. The bell rings as the bird flies. This sound lets the falconer know where the bird is.

Bird of pray

In the Middle Ages the merlin was known as the ladies' falcon, probably because it is so small. Some ladies even took their merlins to church with them!

The secretary bird

The secretary bird has the longest legs of any bird of prey. It stalks the African plains looking for food, walking as much as 30 km a day.

High dives
When trying to attract a mate the secretary bird does a little dance on the ground. It also makes wonderful acrobatic flights, climbing up high and then dropping down from the sky.

Claim to fame
The secretary bird's long legs make it the tallest bird of prey. It eats all sorts of creatures but is famous for hunting snakes. Tough scales on its legs protect the secretary bird against poisonous snakebites.

Tree-top homes
Secretary birds build large nests on the top of flat-topped trees, such as thorn trees. They usually lay only two eggs. Parents take turns hunting for food and guarding the nest. These parents are changing shifts for nest-sitting duty.

It's a birdie!
Snakes are not the secretary bird's only prey. It will eat insects, mammals, birds, eggs, and the occasional small tortoise – whole. One was even known to eat a golf ball!

The bird raises its crest of black feathers when excited and when attracting a mate

Snake snack
The secretary bird uses its very strong legs to kill a snake. It stamps on the snake and then stabs the snake with its back talon.

Glamorous looks
The secretary bird has a brightly coloured face and wonderful eyelashes which are almost 2 cm long.

Index